CONTINUOUS CREATION

Poetic Sequences

BY

ADRIAN ROGERS

ISBN: 978-93-6354-785-8

First Edition: 2026
Rs. 200/-

Cyberwit.net
HIG 45 Kaushambi Kunj, Kalindipuram
Allahabad - 211011 (U.P.) India
http://www.cyberwit.net
Tel: +(91) 9415091004
E-mail: info@cyberwit.net

Printed at Repro India Limited.

Contents

PART 1—BY THE HOURS OF DAY AND NIGHT

PRIME—THE FIRST HOUR

I sing the dawn—bell tone
of a rising sun
Prime, the prayer
of greeting a new day,
having begun
that long procession of light
resonating
through the powers of creation.

A world, re-born up-rises
under the bright
burning eye of one
who, heralding 'the sun
behind the sun'
is beyond time, and even
the infinite.

"*Lift up your hearts*"
let hours pass
we play our parts,
time's shadow darts
mood-changing
blue mountain slopes,
waterways flash-whitening,
rhymes and tropes
for all who...as children
of the sun are born of light.

TERCE—THE THIRD HOUR

Three hours from dawn
and horses of the sun
pace an arc of sky
sun-fired, sparking
chariot wheels, rising
along a limitless
blue-burning track
towards meridian triumph,
echo-sounding,
summoning—light born
a resonance, begun
yet tested by a splendour
chanted, praising
multi-colored glories
earth-wide expanses,
ploughlands, pastures,
forests, mountains,
seas...swarming towns
and cityscapes.

The solar charioteer
looks up—along
a light-born ray
his burning arc a track,
a timeless way
towards eternity.

SEXT—THE SIXTH HOUR

I am 'meridian', timed
transient, song-chimed
preparing—rhymed
ascending
yet inevitably destined
tracking...
towards evening,
but 'now', in blazing
momentary glory,
and gold/white beauty's
activating story
is...radiant, yet hazing
a fan-sweep earthwards
over green lands
mountain-slopes
blue-into-purple,
rivers, seas, sparking
a firing of the day's
colorations in loveliness
beyond conceiving
or devising.

Grant me—the sun
a kingdom's moments
golden yet whitening,
and a memory's powers
never fading.

NONES—THE NINTH HOUR

The sun's meridian moments
passed me, lit golden
slanting into afternoon
from a silent noon song
echoing...
along a lengthening light
unto the ninth hour.

Meridian
was a time of stillness
before—with slower pace
passing on
into Nones—a time of grace,
remembered
as a pulse-beat in the chant—
"Seven times a day
Do I praise Thee..."
exalted as—
"Creation's secret force",
and a wide-spanning sun
sinking slowly
over green lands glowing,
as I recall
that warm ninth hour
of long descent, to evening
and the lighting of the lamps.

VESPERS—THE EVENING OFFICE

A lengthening light fade's
red-flushed quietness
is sunset,
in-gathering outplayed breezes
in a fullness
of momentary peace,
a release
from tension after toil
as lights blink-in, a foil
to restlessness.

Ducks overfly
a slightly rippled lake
in a sprayed-off shake
of the day, winging,
towards a nesting island.

To what then
has the day amounted
to be counted
for a last-light peace,
an orderly singing
of Vespers—
"Hail gladdening light!"
a reflective rest
for the soul, or a test
of peacefulness
in flickering candle flames?

COMPLINE—THE NIGHT OFFICE

From the ends of the earth
we call—
bidding a blessing at nightfall.

Herself a new birth, night,
to the soul—
is wisdom's perfect sphere,
a goal,
a wonder…calling clear
into the dark
as a monotoned bell-toll
calmly setting
a processional night's pace
to Compline,
pure sublimity, grace,
lamps lit
in a sacred space,
'before the ending of the day'
…in peace.

Chanting voices release
the day, as we depart
leaving one lamp lit,
but who…
will keep vigil with me,
'til dawn?

THE GREAT SILENCE

A slow—
rundown timing
after Compline…is
whispers echoing
in vaulted spaces,
slow-pulsed graces
following
shadowed faces
of friends.

What begins, ends,
paring-back
to essentials,
closing…the track
to sleep
as candles blink out.

Let there be—
no troubled dreams,
no futuristic
febrile schemes
hounding the moment,
instead,
closure, contentment,
release,
surcease…

The Great Silence.

THE NIGHT VIGIL

We...lone vigil keepers
through hours long
the heart strong
may endure,
unveil consciousness.

Do you remember
when summer days
seemed endless?

I am content
with a single light,
a stone-dark cell,
unrelenting quietness,
no bell...of release.

Let there be—
no betrayal by friends,
a love that never ends,
hopes remembered,
no tokens dismembered,
just silence,
thoughts stilled,
minds willed—to peace,
time slow-pulsed,
released
in one light burning low,
until the dawn...

PART 2—THE MYSTIC ROSE

ONE LIGHT, ONE VIGIL...

...one flame in the dark,
one point of focus,
one mark
these...the locus
of my hopes,
a sensing of the spark
...about to fall,
a call—to be followed
through cold and dark
enclosed by a wall
of silence,
night's chill deepening
challenging
testing vision.

Watchman, what of the night?

Is it...looking back
outstretched on the rack,
a shafting light
piercing the night
echoing like a toned bell,
a door
swung wildly open...not,
onto a floor
of burning stars
but into the Paradise Garden,
and the Mystic Rose?

THE MYSTIC ROSE

The Rose is a mystery
long years hidden,
a splendour, a story
from the distant past,
a singing bidden
in valleys blue/veiling
the mountains
of western China.

A slender beginning,
a journey of loving,
a sacrificial winning
tested by the Dove
descending
strongly intending to
peace…was release,
from powers outspent
in coloured diversity,
red, white, faceted,
masquerading,
clustered, unforgetting,
for she—Rosa Mystica
is mystery indwelling.

LOTUS

Flower of light
no power of night
can forestall the day,
no dark ray
on time's polluted waters
or swamps of unreason
defy the current,
or counteract seasons
of consciousness,
the incense of dreams
as the sun casts
bright slanting beams
enchanted…
across a night-dark vision
beyond time and place.

Queen of water lilies
no power
can touch your jewel-white
loveliness
no Gordian Knot of scheming
cut away
or veil the numinous
because…
love's golden autumn
elevates your brightness
beyond time's transience
into the timeless.

BLUEBELLS

Voices on the breeze,
spring voices,
songs echoing
sights, sounds, choices,
lengthening days
colouring in light rays,
grounding
perception's being,
processed…
through leaf-filtered
lightness, springing
wherever a singing
green/gold brightness
is a tale told,
carpeted by bluebells
calling…
softly ring-dancing
blue-nodding heads,
clustering,
delicately tossing
in woods green-glowing
spring-lightening
as I walk the paths
of bluebells, blessing
each day, messaging
their glory, their song,
our story.

WALK TO THE PARADISE GARDEN

Wild, overgrown,
a memory of Paradise?
Walk with me
to the Paradise Garden
beyond times, seasons,
reasons, the chimes
of distant bells.
the river, silver-glinting,
everlasting afternoon
unwinding…
through a hidden valley
green-across, widening
with flags yellow/growing
along riverbanks,
gold kingcups, floating
in crystalline shallows.

All seasons lead on, past
early white snowdrops,
golden crocuses,
daffodils yellow/trumpeting,
red and white roses
wild/running, climbing,
a river running slow,
caressing green banks,

so…shall we stay
in this paradise dream,
or be 'passers-by'.

PART 3—THE LONG ESCAPE; NARRATED IN NINE POEMS.

1-THE CHALLENGE OF THE TUNDRA

We sought a full escape
from Arctic tyranny,
that flight might be the shape
of things to come,
for two souls the sum
of aspiration in harmony
with one another,
Katarina and myself—
not sister and brother
but two who loved each other.

With snows melting
from mosses, lichens
summer/green, and blue
starlike Tundra flowers,
we shouldered our crosses
in hope…taking flight
by summer's light,
crossing the tundra
by reindeer tracks, with furtive
arctic fox and shadow-silent
snowy owl
…but the Tundra deceived.

Moss/lichen green
and variegated heath
were soft surfaced
but perma-frosted beneath,
the hidden hardness

of a trodden way
over oozing spongy ground
innocent-seeming
under a thin-bright arctic sun.
Days unfolded as we trod
the weathered sod
winter-free, yielding
yet tiring underfoot.
Arctic Fox
had shed his winter white
flitting by dun-colored,
speculatively watching
for silvery/grey
mindless lemmings,
…until we saw
a long, dark forest line
crossing the horizon
southward, dead ahead.

We had sheltered
with reindeer herders
at their summer pastures
shielded from pursuit,
and brother Wolf, we knew
would never harm us
on the long-lit days,
but shadowy warning signs
could not be gainsaid,
exhaustion—
the inevitable offshoot
of gulag tyranny…

2-WARNING SIGNS

...until we approached
that dark forest line
crossing the horizon
southward...

"Katarina, you're tired.
Think you I do not know
an arctic gulag's
cold-iron tyranny
leaves none, unharmed?"

In the cool sobriety
of green-dimmed forest light
a shy sika deer glided
soft-footed in emanating
quietness, hardly disturbing
a faint breeze sighing
among branches drooping.
Ahead, tall columned
long-straight trunked trees
lordly seeming, stood,
a ranking forest cathedral
spanning infinite distances.

"'Tis true, my love,
tiredness oppresses
body, but not soul.
Freedom is a goal
worth all our striving,
so let us be ongoing."

3—FOREST JOURNEY

Forests can be wild
storm and fire scourged,
but we were blest
with peace, under trees
tall whispering, speaking
gently, yet through shadows
lengthening, reminding us
that all things pass away.

Forest people helped us
with food, shelter, and
that kindness shown
so often to fugitives
from oppression, as lynx,
bear, wolf, and deer
became—silently, yet
speaking our companions,

watched over…
by the Amur Leopard
with his spotted coat,
and once, seen distantly
through looming trees
the long-striped form
of a shadowing tiger,
until we reached
the forests' ending
out-stepping onto
wide, green/rolling
Mongolian grasslands.

4—SHADOWS ACROSS THE LIGHT

The Steppe was wild green
vastness, a limitless sheen,
endless horizons, horses,
cattle, nomad herders
...but Katarina
could walk no further.
She had been longer
in the merciless gulag's
tyranny than I...
"Sit on that fallen tree, my love.
I will seek help."

Herders saw us.
little knew I of their tongue
but, with signs, enough.
Katarina could not ride
unaided, so I mounted,
they passed her up to me
then led us to their camp
and carried her gently
into the Shaman's yurt.

What could I say...?

"Father, Shaman,
please heal her.
we are fugitives, and I
have nothing to offer
but my fears, my tears,
and my love."

5—THE VIGIL

Night crept softly
from the west, beyond
the thin lamp-lighting
of the yurt.
The Camp quietened
as stars whitened
awakening the night,
but Katarina
in a feverish dream
was restless, yet
unawakening.

The Shaman sought
to heal her, by his arts
call…but she, far gone
could little longer stay.

"Brother," he whispered
"The gulag has done
its evil work,
I cannot hold her long.
She might stay
another day, but you
must be prepared
to let her go.
Look now beyond
our little light, the stars
are calling,
another day, a night,
no more…"

6—SING HER TO THE STARS

Another day she lingered
on the threshold
between one moment
and the timeless,
at times unconscious,
then her eyes would open
and she looked at me
unspeaking,
yet with love beyond
the need for words.

The life of the camp
flowed on, but detached
was I from living,
until evening crept in
quietening the moments
of lamp-lighting.

She woke—
reaching for my hand,
waiting, on the edge
of time's long strand.
Night, had descended into
stillness…
then her hand left mine.

The Shaman whispered,
"Come, brother, sit with me,
and we will sing her
to the stars."

7—ALONE

Remembering—
is pain, sharper
than a thorn-sharp sedge,
yet a summary
of voice and love
flowering into memory.

Grasslands fade
into sand, scrub, and
beige-pale thornbush
when I recall—stayed
and heart-strong
yourself...in a rush
of undying love.
Now bereft I must go on,
fulfilling our quest.
Be with me, my love
as by sun and stars
I endure the test
of a long pilgrim road,
your love my goad
as I shoulder
the pack-load of living.

I know you are watching
from the stars
as my heart—catching
each footstep
holds you—in the vase
of undying love.

8—TO THE MOUNTAINS FEET

I walked in a wilderness
of soul and spirit
yet quickened pace
and the grace
of love's long memory,
Katarina's essential self
reaching out to me,

in a landscape's low-lying
monotony,
saltbush, sand, thorns
desolated—earth-dry,
where the wind's low sigh
tuned camel bells
of trading caravaners,
and grateful was I
for kindness around
campfires...until

in the light of a dawn
cold-clear ahead
I saw mountains stark
in first light...dark
lightening to blue/grey,
snow-capped-shining
sun-sparking,
and others gathered
waiting for freedom,
their faith and fellowship
a remembrance of her.

9—TO FREEDOM

I stood between
shadowed spurs of rock
thrust northward to the plain
as the Morning Star dipped
and the Sun rose
to unlock another day.
Ahead…
pine/clad mountain slopes
were cleft—on a light ray
by a green valley,
a waterflow clear glittering
in the dawn sun,
and a holy silence.

I was called, with others
to follow on
where she would have trod
with those gone before
on that same quest
for freedom in the spirit
that priceless gift
of the Divine Architect,
to hear again
the Shaman's voice
from far back on the plain:
"Turn your eyes again
when night comes on,
northward—to the Pole Star
and know…
that she has never left you."

PART 4—WINGS OF MYSTERY

ARCTIC TERN

Black-capped/white breasted
sky-born wanderer,
wind-wave challenger,
spinning earth
and storm-wild seas
are far below your soaring
grey-winged shadow
destined to be—
a tested a wind-rider
wave-gliding, storm defying.

You mobbed me
on a Shetland summer day
above a grass/ground nest
valiant against greater powers,
defending
your young from wing-wild
thieving,
while the sun danced
on shadow-shortened
grey-tapering wings,
and you configured
the sea's unpredictable moods,
across skies
blue or grey/clouded,
leaving a northern winter
for the refuge
of Kakadu's yellow waters
under the sun
of a southland summer.

WANDERING ALBATROSS

White-winged wanderer
yours be the sea-sky spaces
soaring graces
Southern Ocean grandeur,
wing-backed sweeping
awake or sleeping
challenging the thunder
of long-backed rollers
one thousand miles from land
or breakers dissolving
onto distant shores
actualizing—
through perception's doors
endlessly grand
globe-spanning mysteries
beyond times, places,
and histories.

May world-roaming sailors
remember,
but not—like the Ancient Mariner
dismember
the iron rule of destiny,
ignoring
their customary homage
to the wild-winging Albatross
outriding
the long trade winds,
wanderers guiding, oceans
mastering.

SNOWY OWL

Spirit of the Arctic,
under your wing shadow
the swift sweep
of a long-glide-flight
is time's window…onto
a world silent
as the snow falling
from a winter-hard sky.

White angel of silent death
evoking
the biting ice breath
unrelenting
as a blade-sharp arctic wind,
hunting
the far north, magically
haunting
as a green, fan-sweeping
aurora borealis
ruling the polar dark…

I saw you—
under an overcast stark
perched on rocks
at the limit of your range,
a moment…watchful,
changeless,
then gone.

WHITE DOVE—THE MESSENGER

My wings catch the sun
in a dawn-lit shimmer,
my olive leaf hope's glimmer
to a questing Noah
as the floods go down,
I, who have perched
on the shoulder
of Fair Melusine
Grail Maiden and Queen.

I am her messenger—
'My Lady of the Waters',
I summon Parsifal,
Bors, Galahad,
Time's sons and daughters
questing for the Grail,
daring to shake
the foundations of mystery.

I am promise and story,
untamed forces, a glory
of sweeping wings,
so come, if you speak
for 'The desire of nations,'
offer oblations
to Fair Melusine,
Grail Maiden and Queen.

WHITE EAGLE OF THE SUN

Winter sun is a sharp glare
on a frosted landscape,
a perceived share
of glancing shadows,
memories caught then lost
in a mindscape.

White Eagle is prophecy,
mystery, what may be
beyond winter's low-lit story
and a frost-bitten tree.

From the world's far side
White Eagle is a guide
over-flying…
sea-wild expanses,
sense-overriding
the detritus of pride,
gliding the frivolous
moment, predating hopes,
following those Magi
questioning
a light in the sky
not knowing why, only
that a birth must be…?

From whither,
along the roads of life
comes 'The Child of Our Time,
shattering liberal illusions?

WEDGE-TAILED EAGLE

The eyes of a watcher
scan the Outback,
the passings
of living things, close,
averse, time-distant,
instant,
stretched on the rack
of suspenseful waiting,
overseeing
sand-dusted veiling
or unveiling mysteries,
impartial histories
of earth, rock—cold
or sun-scorched
wide-plain or hill-eroded
in a weathering
enigma's decoding.

The searching gaze
of a wedge-tailed eagle
is impartial,
a true *Draconarius,* regal,
imperial, possessive,
reflecting…the seen
and unseen
beneath a burning sky,
whereunder all things
live and die.

PART 5—MEMORIES AND SYMBOLS

IRON CROSSES

Let me clasp His garment's hem
that I may never forget them.

Iron crosses
are standing strong
for those who long
to be remembered,
lives dismembered
by hunger.
Who has counted
their losses, since,
discounted
they caused little stir
in the halls of power?

They did not cower—
from youth's flower
to age's dower,
seeking only justice,
facing eviction
starvation, injustice,
lost hopes…death
taking the last breath
of opportunity.

Let me clasp His garment's hem
that I may never forget them.

SHADOW AND LIGHT

Long-cast shadow
and light,
seasons, footmarks,
dew-wet sun-sparks
or dry sands
away/swept, dusted
by the wind, are…
what insight remembers,
discerns or dismembers,
the real—
from the unreal,
but we are more…than
ships that pass in the night.

When I see you, I recall—
the long light/fall
of an enchanted sunset,
the echo-ringing
musical call
of a reed-haunting bird,
a gliding swan,
a tranced stillness
over the lake…

and these, being true
are enough,
because they are you.

TREE DREAMS—WILLOW MAGIC

My roots are river washed,
my branches overhang
her rippling flow,
leaves green/shadowing
the waters…sway
in a skittering breeze
on the river's dancing-run,
her destiny long since begun
to mirror passing time.

I watch river traffic
pulsing hours in a chime
of busy-ness, and Druids
with my bark subduing pain,
but my darkness few mark
for I am ancient
beyond gain of years,
roots grasping,
trunk gnarled,
branches flexed, skeletal,
whispering…
in dark-forested liturgies,
echoing…
a sacrificial calling.
"Follow me not
into Nemet's mysteries
but be content with sun,
shade, and green-long days."

TREE DREAMS—COCONUT PALM

My clustered, long
yet delicate fronds
green graciously
the shorelines
of a thousand islands,
tossing…
in mild sea breezes
singing…
their elegant, wide
enchanting songlines
sweeping…
above a low lifting
sun-sparked ocean,
dancing…gold on blue.

I am the food
of island nations,
my milk sustains
the coruscating energies
of youth…and,
though I endure
both storm and calm
my chant—'a charm
of lullabies'
shadow-guides, in low
red-glancing sunsets
far outspread
the passing years.

STARSHINE

Across limitlessly
black-pulsed skies
stars blink,
distantly sharp-bright
as if in flight
from perceived desires
to know the stories
of their star-fires.

The Southern Cross
uplifting...below
an equatorial zone
of mystery
transcends perceptions,
time/space crossing
revealing
Ant-ilia the Air Pump,
Apus, dazzling
Bird of Paradise
glorifying Ara
on the Altar of Time
and eternity,
half revealing Sirius
in diamantine sublimity
where Antares the red
closes on Achemar
blue/white, supreme.

CHARIOT OF THE SUN

Helios reins-in
his Chariot of the Sun,
a pride of horses
having begun
their charge, sparking
a harnessed ride,
rising, sweeping,
drawing, leaping wide,
soaring towards
the horizon's rim…

an exultant hymn
to a blazing dawn's
light waves overrunning
greens, browns,
purpled hills,
weathered moorlands,
ploughlands,
louring mountains,
spread-lighting lakes,
rivers, seas,
desert sandscapes,
time-desolate landscapes,
freshness and new birth.

So be it, blue-white skies
and the prize…
a Bacchanalian festival.

L'Apres-midi d'un faune

Among fields of corn
L' Apres-midi-d'un faune
is—having and being
silently dreaming
erotica…concealed
in woodlands, wildlands,
exotica, farmlands, more
than usual afternoons,

human, animal,
vegetable, mineral,
a moment's summary,
inventory, desiring,
his…is a flummery
of dashingly transient
imagery.

Under overhanging
willows weeping,
reed-tangled, among
bordering grasses,
river-whisperings
at his back…is he
Cupid, Eros, watching
the white slipping
slide of a flute,
hearing, imaging
his nymph of dreams?

MIDDAY FANTASIA

Helios dominates
at the day's height
challenging
ploughland, pasture,
moorland, desert,
water-springing
un-trammelling
light's intensity
bold-white vestured,
absolute over skyscapes
earth-scapes, seas,
deserts,
none burning wings
on approach
as he sings
transcendent powers.

Streets may shade
but not disempower
or degrade
his hold over land
and water, flaying,
dominating,
until Helios, impelled
turns his chariot back,
riding across
the afternoon hours
into evening.

PART 6—CONTINUOUS CREATION

FROM WHERE COMES THE DAWN...

Over longest
east/rising mountain ranges
ringing the changes
shadowed, white/sparking
in a soaring sun,
from seas where to have
yet be unbonded
by sun-marking
horizons—takes longest
in high-focussed first light,
as green pillared
branching tree networks
light-flickering images
flash...light
patterning over lake
and river constantly rippling,
streaming pearl-silvered
down a waterfall
merge...dissolving, hurled
in a thunderous, torrential
downpour...
to slow wake a town's
city-scaped hazes, mazes
of roofs and towers.

Shouldering black clouds
'Thor's Hammer'
forges, firing, lighting
the dawn—sequentially,
together yet merging.

ROSE WINDOW IN THE DAWN

Eastward…
out of the vaulted dark
dawn-light breaks,
piercing the branding mark
of a defeated Cain
as pride is shaken,
and night gives place
with shimmering grace
to a Rose Window's
radiant blaze
dispersing the haze
breaking…into mystery,
flowers, angels, apostles,
prophets, heroes
dancing in a rising sun
paraded…consecrated,
manifested,
divinely sparked,
radiant in splendour,
a multi-faceted trumpeting
across golden light
released…

She…is The Rose,
the window's heart,
a glory, the whole,
yet part of all that is
and I…salute her!

SEASHORE SUNRISE

A moment's perception
and a seashore sunrise
is a flare of light,
a becoming prize
first—since the inception
of being...
into time and space.

Scattered shells
and wet-dry sands
throw-back light, sparked,
blazing.

Creation's point-marked
interpreting...of
A who-dares wins
eye/mind opening
is a seeing ceremony
of divestment, snake-like,
sloughing-off its skin.

Creation's morning
beside the borders
of the white-winging sea
is a waiting—other time,
a sacred rhyme linking life
with...*the silent dawn.*

A SONG OF THE HIGH HILLS—AFTER DELIUS

From valley floors
surrounding hills
are green-long sweeps
and awareness in leaps
opening doors
to infinite perceptions,
vistas changing
like seekers grasping
immensities
immeasurable
above and beyond
the illimitable.

Birds wheeling
glide across interspaces,
sun/shafting,
flash-dancing
incessantly aerial ballets,
until evening's
summer-slow descent
calls them…
to dreamscapes
light-drifting
down wide/wild slopes
at days…ending.

SCAPEGOAT FOR JUSTICE

Dune-waves golden
burn—under a pitiless sky,
sand is grit beneath feet.

Gazing ahead
in a meridian's heat
as horizons shimmer,
turning, head bowed,
facing rocks red/jagged,
wind blasted…
I am fated to wander.

Light, lovely at dawn
pearled into evening
is but a summoning.
Are there green palms,
crystalline waters, charms
of an evening at rest?

I have done nothing
to justify abandonment,
but the Priest Kind came
with halter and chain,
dragging me to the farce
of a trial.

Why then, this pretence
of atonement?

MEMORIAL GARDEN—LAE, PAPUA NEW GUINEA

Through a gate,
from the town's bustle
we passed
to a quiet, devotional
timelessness...aware
of open spaces,
well mowed greenness,
orderly graces,
a long, tree-crowned
embankment
verdant yet restrained,
flower-plantings
red, yellow, blue, pink
leading on...
to the Cross of Sacrifice,
Lae's tribute
to those who gave all
for this town.
Passing a grave
we read—
aged seventeen years.
"You're only boys—
some of you. You should be
readying your futures,
not here!"

"...but we are awaiting
a new dawning."

WILD RIVER

I am from the Source
untamed—
beauty, power,
creation unconfined,
free—within the mind
of nature
to suppress or redirect,
birthing
a racing torrent's flashing
dancing
diamantine sparking
sunlit rapids,
crashing
over ridge-toothed rocks
leaping
over river-worn blocks,
singing mysteries,
levelling off, slowing,
breaking free—
beyond dawn's thunder,
a meridian sun's blessing,
deepening,
parading nature's power.
Creation—
I endower…daylong,
nightlong, forever!

ANOTHER MERIDIAN

The solar chariot's horses
dance…a meridian slope
ascending
under the glance of Helios
at the peak of day
across land, and stilled
or flowing waters.

The chance taken
—is a dawn-sprung trope,
a versifying
by the Charioteer
styling his horses to prance
upon a light ray.

One in a band
divinely companioned,
empowered,
of sons and daughters
endowered,
he takes his solar throne
presiding—
over lands green,
many-coloured, waters
blue and silvered, until time
demands
his chariot's downward turn
to evening.

EPILOGUE—ON THE MARCH

WER'E MARCHING STILL

...from the Slipper Chapel
where a lamp burned low
in the dark
before dawn came, slow.
We pilgrims laid aside
our shoes
and rhythmic trappings
of existence
with a tried insistence
on divesting
outer selves, marching
one last mile to the Shrine,
investing
each, in self-awareness,
singing
in the dark-before dawn
silence...

Until the dawn, my friends
until the dawn,
we march, we stumble
one last mile to the Shrine
for healing at the Spring,
we do not grumble,
or denigrate the sting
of cut and tired feet,

We're marching still...

www.ingramcontent.com/pod-product-compliance
Ingram Content Group UK Ltd.
Pitfield, Milton Keynes, MK11 3LW, UK
UKHW041316190726
13845UKWH00025B/308

9 789363 547858